W9-BFC-150

DATE DUE

HOW

HISTORY OPENS WINDOWS

THE ANCIENT CHINESE

JANE SHUTER

Heinemann Library
Chicago, Illinois

Color Reproduction by Dot Gradations, England

Printed in Hong Kong, China

Produced by Celia Floyd

04 03 02 01
10 9 8 7 6 5

Library of Congress Cataloging-in-Publication Data

Shuter, Jane.
    The ancient Chinese / Jane Shuter.
        p.   cm. -- (History opens windows)
    Includes bibliographical references and index.
    Summary: An introduction to the various elements of ancient
Chinese civilization, including great thinkers, family life, inventions,
and the government.
    ISBN 1-57572-593-2 (lib. bdg.). --ISBN 1-57572-594-0 (pbk.)
    1. China--Civilization--Juvenile literature.   2. China--History–
Juvenile literature.   [1. China–Civilization.]   I Title. II. Series.
DS721.S488   1998
951--dc21   97-35801
                                                                        CIP
                                                                        AC

Acknowledgments

The author and publishers are grateful to the following for permission to
reproduce copyright photographs:

Ancient Art & Architecture Collection Ltd., p. 7, 12, 27; Bibliotheque Nationale,
Paris, p. 8; British Museum, p. 10, 13, 14, 16, 17, 20, 28; Smithsonian, Freer Art
Gallery, Washington DC, p. 18, 26; The Museum of Fine Arts, Boston, p. 21; WM
Rockhill Nelson Gall, p. 22; National Palace Museum, Taiwan, p. 24.

Cover photograph © Ancient Art & Architecture Collection Ltd.

Every effort has been made to contact copyright holders of any material
reproduced in this book. Any omissions will be rectified in subsequent printings
if notice is given to the publisher.

Some words are shown in bold, **like this**. You can find out what they mean
by looking in the glossary.

Contents

Introduction

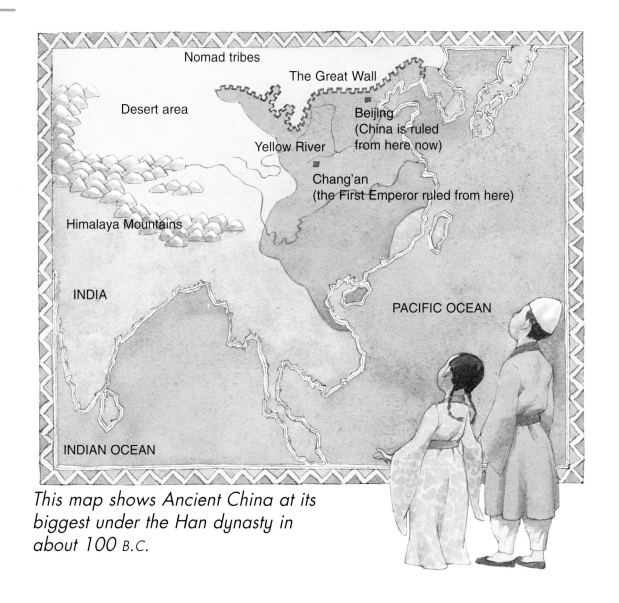

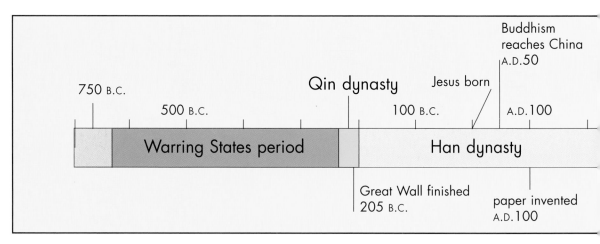

This map shows Ancient China at its biggest under the Han dynasty in about 100 B.C.

Labels on map:
- Nomad tribes
- The Great Wall
- Desert area
- Beijing (China is ruled from here now)
- Yellow River
- Chang'an (the First Emperor ruled from here)
- Himalaya Mountains
- INDIA
- PACIFIC OCEAN
- INDIAN OCEAN

Timeline:
- 750 B.C.
- 500 B.C.
- Qin dynasty
- Jesus born
- 100 B.C.
- Buddhism reaches China A.D.50
- A.D.100
- Warring States period
- Han dynasty
- Great Wall finished 205 B.C.
- paper invented A.D.100

People first lived in China about 500,000 years ago. They hunted and then farmed along the Huang He (pronounced "hwong hee"), also called the Yellow River. Historians divide ancient Chinese history into dynasties, which are blocks of time when China was ruled by different families. Each dynasty is named after the ruling family.

The first two Chinese dynasties, the Shang and the Zhou (pronounced "Jo"), ruled from 1700 B.C. to 770 B.C. But the Zhou dynasty lost control. Families that ruled different parts of China fought for power. This period, called the Warring States, lasted 600 years. Finally, the Qin (pronounced "chin") dynasty won. From then on, China was ruled by one Chinese dynasty after another until the Mongols invaded in 1279.

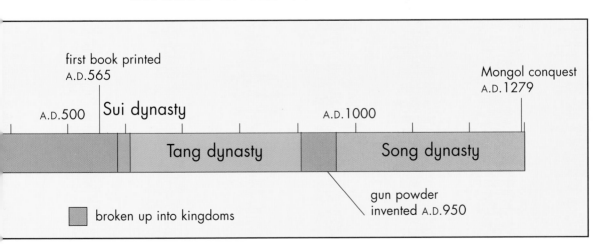

first book printed
A.D. 565

Mongol conquest
A.D. 1279

A.D. 500   Sui dynasty   A.D. 1000

Tang dynasty   Song dynasty

broken up into kingdoms

gun powder
invented A.D. 950

The First Emperor

The First Emperor wanted a great burial. For years before his death, workers made a huge terra-cotta [pottery] army to guard his tomb. Here they are making horses.

Shi Huangdi (pronounced "She hwong dee"), leader of the Qin, renamed himself "the First **Emperor**" because he wanted his dynasty to make a new start after the Warring States period. His **empire** was bigger than any earlier empire. He was the first ruler to try to make China one country.

Earlier rulers had let different parts of their empire live differently. The First Emperor did not. He made people use the same writing, the same coins, and the same weights and measures in the markets. He even made them make carts the same size to fit the new roads being built all over the empire.

Here are a few of the 7,000 terra-cotta warriors who guarded the First Emperor's tomb. They were made with great care. No two of them are exactly the same.

How China was Ruled

The First **Emperor** wanted to control the **empire**. So he set up a system of officials to run the country. There were officials to run the army and also officials to organize common citizens. These officials collected **taxes**, checked markets, and punished criminals. This system was used for many years. Only men could become officials. They had to pass a set of tests held every three years. For each person who passed, about 3,000 failed.

This painting shows the First Emperor reading the results of a test to become a government official.

In ancient China, the emperor was
the most important person. He owned
all the land. Everyone had to obey him.
After him came the **nobles**. These were
rich and important Chinese families.
Next were scholars, who studied
and wrote books—education and
knowledge were very important to the
ancient Chinese. Next came the farmers
who kept everyone fed. The least
important people were shopkeepers,
craftworkers, and then **merchants**.

*Only an
emperor's
family, nobles,
and important
officials could
talk directly
to him.*

9

Religion

Ancient Chinese religion had many different parts. Sometimes it is hard to separate them from each other. One of the most important parts for many common people involved the spirits and demons that affected everyday life.

There were spirits of nature and of different parts of life, such as wealth, health, children, and happiness. All these spirits had to be kept happy.

The Guardian King of the North controlled the north point of the compass. He was just one of the many spirits and demons that could change everyday life.

A huge statue of Buddha, carved into the mountain for people to worship at.

The ancient Chinese also worshipped the spirits of their parents, grandparents, great-grandparents, and other **ancestors**. On special days in spring and autumn, everyone spent time at **temples** or family shrines to worship their ancestors.

From the first century A.D., the emperors were interested in Buddhism. They heard about it by trading with India, where Buddhism began. Buddhists believed in **meditation** and **reincarnation**.

Great Thinkers

Confucius taught in about 500 B.C. He told people how to behave. Confucius also believed that the past was important. The First **Emperor** burned Confucius' writings because he wanted to make a new start. Years later, followers of Confucius spread his teachings. Confucius' ideas became popular once again.

One of his most important ideas was that a person should obey and respect people who are older and more important.

Lao Tzu (Lao rhymes with "cow," and Tzu is pronounced "Sue") lived at about the same time as Confucius. He told people to **meditate** on the "Tao," or "Way." He said all living things should work together in harmony.

Confucius said every group of people, from families to countries, had to follow this rule: "obey more important people and take care of less important people."

Lao Tzu's ideas about the Way, or Tao, later became a religion called Taoism.

Country Life

Most common Chinese people lived and worked in the countryside. They grew different crops, depending on the weather. In the north they grew grain, like wheat and **millet**. In the south where it was wetter, farmers grew rice. Most people grew vegetables and kept chickens and pigs. Oxen and buffalo pulled their plows and carts.

In spring, the **emperor** was the first to plow a field. This showed that farming was very important. But even though farmers were important to the **empire**, they were usually the poorest people in it.

Rice must be underwater for part of its growing time, so rice fields need to be near rivers. Here farmers move water from the river to the paddy field with a bamboo scoop.

14

HOW

Ancient
Chinese

A guarded village from the time of the First Emperor.

This cart belongs to
the lord because it is
pulled by horses.
Common villagers
might share one or
two buffaloes or
oxen to pull their
carts and plows.

Common people
live in these one
roomed thatched
houses.

The well is where all
the water comes
from, including
drinking water for
humans and animals.

The lord of
the land all
around the
village has
a house in
this village.

15

Town Life

The size and design of cities showed how powerful an **emperor** was. New emperors often had a capitol city built to rule from. These cities were carefully planned, with the emperor's palace and the government offices at the end farthest from the poor parts of the city.

Other cities and towns were carefully planned too. Many had big market places and special streets set aside for different businesses. Smaller towns grew bit by bit. They had many wood houses on narrow, twisting streets. These houses could catch fire and burn down very easily.

Farmers brought extra crops to market to sell. They shared an ox cart, like the one in this model, to carry the crops.

A busy town market.

This man
has just sold
his sheep.

This man is
telling stories.

Traders have
set up stalls on
the bridge.

People are
dyeing silk in
this workshop.

Villagers without carts
carry baskets on
bamboo poles over
their shoulders.

This scholar makes
his living writing
letters for people.

Family Life

The ancient Chinese had very clear ideas about how a family should live. The father was the head of the family. Everyone had to obey him, even his grown-up children. Confucius taught that people should be more respected as they grew older. So the oldest members of the family were well cared for.

Men worked and did business outside the home. Women did not work unless they had to. Most women ran the home and looked after the children. Poor women worked in the fields or as servants in wealthier homes.

Women in rich families had no work to do, but did not often go out. So they had to entertain each other with games, singing, and talking.

The house of a wealthy Chinese family.

Even wealthy people had very little furniture. The furniture, rugs, and wall hangings they did have were made from expensive woods and fabrics.

The house has a strong wood frame, plastered walls, and a tile roof. Poor people often lived in one room with a straw roof.

The overhanging roof keeps the house cool in the heat and lets water run off when it rains.

Children

Children were a great blessing, especially boys. A large family was a good thing, as long as you could feed everyone! Children were brought up to obey adults.

Boys usually followed their fathers' trades. Wealthy families educated their sons to take the tests to become an official. Sometimes a wealthy family paid for an intelligent poor boy to go to school to learn to take these tests.

This painting shows a man, his wife and children, and grandchildren. The writing in the middle is a prayer that says: "There will be many more children and grandchildren, though many generations."

Girls were expected to marry, run a home, and have children. Girls from **noble** families might be chosen as one of the **emperor's** many wives. They were well looked after for their entire lives. But they had even less freedom than most Chinese women. They spent almost all their time inside the many palaces that belonged to the emperor.

*The girls in this picture are being shown how to make silk. The Chinese were the first to make silk. **Merchants** who sold it all over the world made a lot of money.*

21

Clothes

Most Chinese people wore the same style of clothes. They wore robes wrapped around and tied at the waist. There were several layers of these robes. The outside layer was always the most beautiful. In summer, the layers were thin. In winter, padding was added between several layers of cloth.

You can see the layers of robes on this statue of a Buddhist priest.

Wealthy people wore long robes made from expensive silk fabrics that were beautifully decorated. There were rules about what colors people could wear. There were special colors for the **emperor**. Poor people wore flat shoes or went barefoot. Wealthy women had their feet bound. Their feet were wrapped tightly in cloth from birth. This broke the bones and made the feet like tiny stumps. Many people thought this looked beautiful.

The emperor and his **nobles** wear richly decorated silk robes. The robes are too long to run or work in. This shows that whoever wears these robes does not work.

The scholar and his wife wear less expensive clothes. But their robes are long, and his shoes have curled toes. They are hard to work or run in.

The farmer's family wear clothes made from inexpensive fabric. These clothes are comfortable to work in.

Food

The food Chinese people ate depended on how wealthy they were.

Poor people did not eat meat every day. They ate chickens when they stopped laying eggs. They also hunted and ate wild animals.

Wealthy people ate many kinds of meat, such as pork, chicken, lamb, and goose. On special occasions, they served more unusual things, like snakes, dogs, snails, and small birds.

Everyone ate vegetables, fruit, and bread. In the south, they ate rice. In the north, people ate a cereal called **millet**. They drank Chinese tea or rice wine. People ate with their fingers or with chopsticks.

These people are eating in a garden. There are many bowls with different foods in them. They will eat with the chopsticks next to their plates.

A food stall in a small town.

Many people in
towns and villages set
up food stalls in the
street. In some towns,
whole streets were
lined with different
food stalls.

This stall owner has
brought a pot of hot
food to sell. Other
stall owners are
cooking over a fire.

This man has
bought a large
meal and is
taking it home
on a tray.

This man has
bought just a
bowl of rice and
is eating it while
sitting on a mat
provided by the
stall owner.

25

Inventions

The Chinese invented and discovered many things. Many of their inventions were very useful, like wheelbarrows and writing paper. They also figured out how to move water for farming and how to predict earthquakes. Other inventions include things that made them stronger in war, such as gunpowder and steel for sharper swords.

It was important to be able to lift water, especially in the south where the rice fields needed flooding at times.

This is a seismographic machine to measure how strong an earthquake is. It was invented by Chang Heng in A.D. 132. When there was an earthquake, balls fell from the dragons' mouths (at the top) into the toads' mouths (at the bottom).

The Chinese also studied the stars and planets. They invented ways of keeping time. Chinese medicine, especially **acupuncture**, is used by more and more people all over the world today instead of modern medicine.

Some Chinese inventions still in use: paper, gunpowder, toilet paper, fireworks, umbrellas, kites, wheelbarrows, **abacuses**, canals, and magnetic compasses.

The Great Wall

The Great Wall was built in the time of the First **Emperor**. It stretched along the northern edge of the Chinese **Empire**. It connected walls built in different places by different dynasties during the Warring States period. The Great Wall was built to keep the Chinese in and the **nomad** tribes that raided from the north out.

The Great Wall was built mostly by the army. Poor farmers and criminals were forced to work on it, too. It was not easy to build. So many people died building it that it was called "the longest graveyard in the world."

A pottery model of a watchtower. Watchtowers were built all along the Great Wall.

The parts of the Great Wall that are left stretch for more than 2,100 miles. Historians think it was even longer when it was first built.

Soldiers guard the wall as it is built. They stop enemies from stealing or breaking down the wall. They also stop workers from running away!

Elephants were brought in to help with moving the heaviest loads. But most of the moving is done by humans.

The Mongol Invasion

By A.D. 1279, the **nomads** in the north, the Mongols, had built themselves into a powerful fighting force. They were building an **empire** of their own. They moved into China and Europe, taking more land than any army before or since. As they took over new lands, they settled and took on the local way of life. Ancient China had come to an end after more than 2,000 years. The Mongol dynasties were just beginning.

Mongol soldiers attack a walled city. They have ladders and a tower to reach the top of the walls.

Glossary

abacuses   devices that use beads to help add, subtract, multiply, and divide

acupuncture   medical treatment in which needles are put into the body at certain points to cure illnesses

ancestors   parents, grandparents, great-grandparents and so on

craftworkers   people who make things for a living

emperor   ruler who has total power, like a king

empire   all the lands controlled by one country

meditation   to think about something in a calm, clear way

merchant   person who buys things from one person and sells them to others

millet   wheat-like grain, used for cooking

nobles   important people

nomads   people who do not live in one place, but move around

reincarnation   belief that a person's soul may be reborn in another body

taxes   money people pay to support their government

temples   places where people worship their gods

More Books to Read

Nicholson, Robert. *Ancient China*. New York: Chelsea House, 1994.

Teague, Ken. *Growing Up in Ancient China*. Mahwah, NJ: Troll Communications, 1993.

Waterlow, Julia. *The Ancient Chinese*. New York: Thomson Learning, 1994.

Index